As Curator of the Carisbrooke Castle Museum, Roy Brinton is an acknowledged authority on the history of the Isle of Wight. He was born on the Island, and joined the local history staff of the Isle of Wight County Council in 1978. He is well-known for his lectures on the Ryde area and as the author of several books on old Isle of Wight illustrations.

E(

1. Frederick Nutt Broderick (1854-1913).

EDWARDIAN ISLAND

The Isle of Wight Photographs of Frederick Broderick

ROY BRINTON

THE DOVECOTE PRESS

First published in 1992 by the Dovecote Press Ltd
Stanbridge, Wimborne, Dorset BH21 4JD

Text © Roy Brinton 1992

Designed by the Dovecote Press Ltd
Photoset by The Typesetting Bureau Ltd, Wimborne, Dorset
Origination by Chroma Graphics (Overseas) Pte Ltd, Singapore
Printed by Kim Hup Lee Printing Co Pte Ltd, Singapore

ISBN 1 874336 02 4

Contents

Introduction

Ryde   5-25

Seaview and St Helens   26-34

Brading and Bembridge   35-44

The Southern Coast   45-55

West Wight   56-64

Cowes   65-72

Newport and Carisbrooke   73-83

Wootton and Havenstreet   84-94

Rural Scenes   95-103

Introduction

Frederick Nutt Broderick came to the Isle of Wight with his parents in 1855, when only a few months old. His father, of the same christian names, was born in Clerkenwell, Middlesex, in 1825 and was a printer and engraver. His mother, Ellen, came from Clapham, Surrey.

It is not known why the family came to Ryde, but possibly they were drawn to the town as it was expanding rapidly and attracting a lot of trades-people from the mainland. Upon arrival, they moved into 10 Cleader Place, a side street near the hospital. They only stayed at this address for a few months, as one of the first Island engravings done by Frederick bears the date June 1856 and the address is 89 High Street, Ryde. This very fine engraving was of the Congregational Chapel, which stood in George Street, Ryde and was burnt down in 1870.

In 1859 the family moved again this time to 1 St Thomas' Square, Ryde, which they rented for £52.10s per annum. The premises over the shop

2. Frederick and his wife Emily in the garden of their home in West Street, Ryde.

and the work areas were extensive with a large drawing room and seven bedrooms. There was to be a need for this size of accommodation, as the Brodericks had seven children.

Frederick, senior, was a supporter of the Liberals and in June 1873 he started printing and publishing a small satirical journal *The Earwig*. It was published monthly and contained cartoons and articles relating to local events.

Frederick junior decided not to follow his father's trade, but to learn a newer form of illustration, photography. By the time he reached the age of 24 he had gone into business alongside his father as a photographer, publishing views of the Isle of Wight.

In 1878 the family decided to give up at St Thomas' Square and moved to Aurora Villa, at the south end of West Street, Ryde. The great snow fall in January 1881 gave Frederick an opportunity to get his photographs widely seen by the public. He photographed nearly all of the main streets of Ryde when they were piled high with snow, and although a fair number have survived, many are faded and therefore it is difficult to obtain a good reproduction.

As the photographic business expanded he took his camera further afield. Prints survive of work done along the south coast, particularly at Hastings where recently a large collection of his postcard negative plates came into the possession of Hastings Central Library. Frederick exhibited in 1876 and 1878 at the Photographic Society of Great Britain, which he joined in 1878. The *British Journal of Photography* made favourable comments on both exhibitions. When the society was granted the prefix of Royal, he was an ordinary member, but became a Fellow in 1895. He also exhibited for the local Mechanics Industrial Society and was awarded a certificate of merit in 1889.

On 7 January 1885 Frederick married Emily Harold at Putney Church. They were to have two

3. The north end of the High Street, Ryde, looking towards St Thomas's Square, following the blizzard in January 1881. In the background can be seen the building marked lithographers, from which Frederick and his father had recently moved in 1878.

daughters, Aurora and Emmeline, born in 1886 and 1888. In the April of the following year Frederick senior died after a long illness, aged 63 years. He was buried in the local Ryde cemetery. In 1903 his widow was interred alongside him.

Frederick junior not only produced local view postcards but also photographic prints for framing or mounting into albums and glass slides for the stereoscope. Various guide book publishers, including Ward Lock, used his photographs to illustrate their works. In 1893 he toured the U.S.A. to see the World's Columbian Exposition at Chicago. He also visited Washington and the Niagara Falls.

In June 1904 Frederick joined a party of tourists going across the Channel and touring France. He took photographs of the trip which he later sold to the tourists. His wife and younger daughter accompanied him to Switzerland in June 1909 and two months later he visited France with his wife and elder daughter.

Frederick continued to operate a very successful business from his home until the end of 1912 when he became unwell. After a long illness he died on 21 November 1913, aged 59. He was buried near his father. His widow, Emily, died in 1918 and was buried with him.

In his obituary it was said that he was a very entertaining lecturer and was in great demand with his lantern and photographic slides, of which he possessed a large number. He was also described as a gentleman of the greatest courtesy.

4. Aurora Villa, West Street, Ryde, to which the Broderick family moved in 1878. The house still stands although it is now divided. In the foreground are Frederick junior's two daughters, Aurora and Emmeline.

His style of photography and the events that he recorded, made him different from most other local photographers. Much of his time was taken up with news photographs recording the celebrations, anniversaries, events and disasters of the time. The prints had to be produced very quickly so that they could be sold whilst the news was still being talked about. This demand for speed sometimes unfortunately led to poor production, and in later years some of the cards became badly faded.

Most photographers concentrated on views for the tourist trade, but Frederick recorded events and celebrations mainly for local people. Because of this only a small number of each was printed and this fact makes his postcards and photographs very collectable today.

It is thanks to Frederick's photographs that we have such a good understanding of what life was like in the Island at the beginning of the century. *Edwardian Island* provides a delightful portrait of the best of his work, and I am indebted to Miss Yvonne Arthur, Mrs Pam Matheson and Mr Ian Murray for kindly allowing me to use photographs from their collections. My thanks are also due to my wife for checking the text and to Mrs Jo Barry for typing it.

ROY BRINTON
Ryde

Ryde

5. By the middle of the 19th century Union Street, Ryde, had become the town's main shopping area. To the left of the photograph, behind the handcart, are the buildings which housed the well known drapery business founded in 1863 by Samuel Fowler. On the roof of the building on the extreme right are the supports of the telephone poles of the local National Telephone exchange. In its first year, 1898, there were 31 subscribers in Ryde but two years later the numbers had risen to 73.

6. December, 1908, was very cold and ended with a heavy snow-storm, as the picture of Union Street shows. Behind the bread delivery boy can be seen the first floor bay windows of the Royal Kent Hotel. One of the early hotels in the town, it was opened in 1835 by Alexander Stephens. Queen Victoria and the Prince Consort stayed there in the mid 1840s.

7. A rare cabinet photograph showing St Thomas's Street, the old road which from early history until the end of the 18th century connected the two communities of Upper and Lower Ryde. The church of St Thomas, with its spire, was built in 1827 on the site of an earlier chapel. To the left is the entrance to Brigstocke Terrace, a terrace of ten large houses built 1826 to 29.

8. In 1908 Ryde Borough Council purchased its first steam fire engine for £326 from Merryweather & Son. On October 9th a large number of people gathered in St Thomas's Square to witness a demonstration of the power of the hoses, which threw jets of water to a height of over 140 feet.

9. The King of Spain and Princess Ena leaving Ryde Town Hall in April 1906 following their engagement in February. The eighteen-year-old Princess was the daughter of Princess Beatrice, Governor of the Isle of Wight and lived with her mother at Osborne Cottage, East Cowes.

10. On New Year's day 1907 the Ryde lifeboat was called out in a storm and capsized. Two of the crew were lost, Henry Howard and Frank Haynes. They were buried in the West Street Cemetary with full honours. In the centre foreground of this sadly rather faded photograph can be seen a sailor carrying the small white coffin of Hayne's baby daughter who died only a few hours before he was called out and was buried with him.

11. Godfrey Baring, a Liberal, beat the Conservative candidate in 1906 by 1,561 votes and thus became M.P. for the Island. Four years later he was defeated. The 'Vote for Baring' hoarding covered the front of the Temperance Hall in Ryde High Street. In the 19th century the building had been a Free-Wesleyan Chapel.

12. Heavy rain in October 1909 led to a local stream bursting its banks and flooding the railway tunnel with some 10 million gallons of water. Steam engines and fire engines, including the Ryde one shown in the photograph, were brought to the tunnel mouth and took six days to pump the water away.

13. Thursday 13 April 1905 was a great day for the Island, for on it a whole new form of transport started, using the very latest motor buses. A fleet of four brand new double decker buses, capable of carrying 36 passengers and operated by the Isle of Wight Motor Express Syndicate, was started by Lady Adela Cockrane, wife of the Deputy Governor of the Isle of Wight. After the opening ceremony the buses went off to Newport, Cowes, Shanklin and Bembridge.

14. The bus waiting-room at 6 Pier Street, between the Albany Hotel and the Wellington Inn. Although the buses had powerful engines they could not cope with the Island roads and hills and had to be withdrawn in the autumn, to be replaced by single deckers. The company struggled on until October 1907, when it ceased to operate due to lack of business. Islanders had to wait until 1922 before they saw an Island-wide service again.

15. DL 78 was one of the four original buses and is seen here in Ryde High Street.

16. *(Below)* The bandstand stood on an area of the Eastern Esplanade which was reclaimed from the sea in 1855 to 57. Some 20 acres were obtained at a cost of £5,000. Between 1869 and 1879 the pier tramway ran across this part of the Esplanade on its way to St John's Road Station.

17. *(Above)* The large dome-shaped pavilion was erected on Ryde Pier Head in 1895 with reading and refreshment rooms attached, close to the tramway station. The pavilion, which could seat a thousand people, was used for concerts, theatricals and entertainments such as this roller-skating Carnival.

18. *(Left)* Western Esplanade, was first proposed in 1877, but it was another 20 years before any action was taken. The local borough council bought four houses which blocked the way from the street to the shore and in 1900 the houses were demolished and construction of the Esplanade finally started. It was opened by Princess Beatrice in 1902.

19. The postman in Upton Road, outside Haylands Post Office (west side) which was in business in 1888 . When this photograph was taken the post-master was Walter Morey, who also had a grocery shop there. The post was collected five times a day on weekdays, the last being 7.40 p.m., and twice on Sundays.

20. Partlands Avenue, Ryde, was laid out 1870-71 and obtained its name from a field in the area. The land on either side of the road was divided into building plots and in 1872 a sewer was laid. The horse and cart are crossing the junction at Swanmore Road with Upton Road to the left, which led to the windmill at Upton Cross.

21. The first windmill was built at Upton, near Ryde in 1529 and was possibly of wooden construction. The stone stump of a later mill can be seen to the right of the windmill. The one shown here was erected in the 19th century and was the largest on the Island. In the early years of this century the miller was Edward Sweetman junior who also had a brewery in Ryde.

22. Maypole dancing during the Childrens' Gala at Ryde House in July 1908. Ryde House was built in the early years of the last century for the lord of the manor, George Player. When this photograph was taken it was the home of his great-grandson William Player Brigstocke. He died in 1929 without issue and the lordship passed to his brother George.

23. Binstead School buildings were erected in 1853 for 146 children; (average attendance 130) at a cost of £525. The site was given by J.Flemming esq., lord of the manor. In the early years of this century the head teacher was George John Springer.

24. Arnold Road, Binstead was built about 1910 and was new when this photograph was taken, with houses on one side only. On the extreme right can be seen the Wesleyan Chapel which was built in 1866 with seating for 150 people.

25. The medieval abbey of Quarr was founded in 1132 and was dissolved by Henry VIII in 1536. The abbey came into the hands of John Mill who demolished most of the buildings, after which the stone was reused for the forts at East and West Cowes and Yarmouth. In the 19th century the site was tidied up and used as a small farm.

Seaview and St Helens

26. Barnsley Harbour, according to the historian Sir John Oglander, was between Springvale and Seaview. It slowly silted up and became a creek with a water mill at the southern end. In the late 18th century the area was sold to the Kirkpatricks and, as salt was a profitable industry, they made the old harbour into a saltern. This photograph shows the cottages built on the east side of the saltern for the workers.

27. When this photograph was taken both the lodge and road at Woodlands Vale to Seaview were new. General Calthorpe, who owned Woodlands Vale estate, decided that the highway was too near the house and in 1898 the local authority allowed him to move the road further away at his expense. The road work was carried out in 1899 and the new entrance and lodge, designed by a local architect, was built in 1900.

28. On the extreme right of this early morning photograph can be seen the entrance to the yard of Edgar Barton, the local coal merchant. His business was at the northern end of Steyne Road, Seaview.

29 & 30. Two photographs of the 'Bathing Ground', Seaview. By the end of the last century bathing machines were starting to go out of use and to be replaced by bathing tents, which quickly became popular as they were portable and easily stored.

31. By the end of the last century Seaview's popularity was assured. This photograph clearly shows the change of attitude towards bathing. In the second half of the last century mixed bathing was not allowed at any of the Island resorts.

32. St Helens Village fair and sports on the green were well established by the middle of the 1800s but declined. Later at the end of the century they were revived and called 'St Helens Annual Sports and Carnival'. The man in the peaked cap, in the middle of the photograph, behind the competitors, is Henry Goodall who started the races with his blunderbuss.

33. In this photograph of the 1908 St Helens sports a young competitor is getting ready to take part. Note the man to his left holding a megaphone.

34. The Territorial Army also held an annual sports day on St Helens Green. In this 1908 photograph the soldiers are manhandling large sacks over a wooden wall. The sacks were loaned by Edward Way & Sons who were the millers at St Helens tide mill.

Brading and Bembridge

35. The medieval town of Brading was accessible by sea before the drainage of the harbour in the 19th century. Its importance can be gauged by the number and size of the buildings in the High Street. The old Town Hall can be seen in front of the church tower. It had brick arches inserted in the 18th century and these gave access to the town's lock-up. In the foreground is a street pump for supplying drinking water to the surrounding houses.

36. *(Left)* According to tradition the first Brading Church was erected in the 7th century, although there is no known trace of it today. The church includes the Oglander chapel which has a fine selection of tombs belonging to the Oglander family. This photograph shows the tower of the church being restored by the Ryde builders, Charles Langdon, in 1906.

37. *(Below)* The bride being led by her father into St Mary's Church, Brading, before a wedding at the turn of the century.

38 & 39. *(Above & opposite page)* Two photographs of West Street, taken in opposite directions, showing the old stone built cottages which were common in Brading. West Street is on the western edge of the town centre and was part of the route from the square to Nunwell, home of the Oglander family who owned most of the land in the area.

40. Situated at the foot of the road from Brading Down to the village is the Congregational Chapel, built of stone in 1847 to seat about 200. In the rear is a small cemetary, which is unusual for Congregationalists, hence many from other parts of the Island are buried here.

41. The railway reached Brading, from Ryde, in August 1864 and the station became a junction in 1882 when a branch line was opened to Bembridge. The photograph shows the station master George Corbett about to hand the staff to a train arriving from Ryde.

42. *(Above)* Elm Cottage, on the outskirts of Brading beside the main road to Ryde. To the right of this narrow road can be seen, in the distance, a steam traction engine, a close up of which is in the adjoining photograph (43). The Wallis & Steepens traction engine is getting ready to haul timber from a field on the Oglander estate.

43. *(Opposite page)* The Wallis and Stevens traction engine just visible on the right in the previous page preparing to haul timber from a field on the Oglander estate. The trees are elm, now sadly almost extinct throughout the Island.

44. Bembridge Railway Station, the terminus of the branch line from Brading, opened in May 1882 after Brading Harbour was reclaimed. The engine was appropriately named *Bembridge* and the notice above the doorway behind the engine states that William Weeks was the station clerk. The large building on the right was the Royal Spithead Hotel, which was built about the same time as the railway.

The Southern Coast

45. Sandown from the pier showing the bathing machines in use towards the end of the 19th century. The ladies' machines can be seen on the left at a discreet distance from the mens'. They were hauled in and out of the water by horses, one of which can be seen tethered on the right. George Hooper and James Newton were the proprietors of the bathing machines.

46. *(Above)* The history of the Isle of Wight Rifles dates from November, 1859 when corps were raised in several towns. These corps acted independently until July 1860 when they were formed into 'The 1st Administrative Battalion, Isle of Wight Volunteers'. Further consolidation came in 1880 when the battalion was renamed 'The Isle of Wight Rifles Volunteer Corps'. For several years before the 1st World War, they held their summer camp at Yaverland, near Sandown Fort.

47. *(Left)* During October, 1909 there were abnormally heavy rains which transformed valleys into lakes, as can be seen in this photograph of Morton Common near Sandown. The flood waters covered the main road from Brading to Sandown. To the right is the embankment which carries the railway line to Sandown.

48. Carnivals have been enjoyed on the Island for many years. They have been keenly supported by the towns-people as much for their own enjoyment, as that of the tourists. This photograph is of a float in the 1905 Shanklin Carnival.

49. The old village at Shanklin was a popular stop on sight-seeing expeditions around the Island. In the background can be seen the Crab Inn, which was always ready to provide refreshment for those passing through the village.

50. In the 1870s the development of the ordinary bicycle, popularly known as the 'penny farthing', led to cycling becoming popular. With the invention, by Kemp Stanley in 1885, of the Rover Safety Bicycle the sport was enjoyed by a lot more people. This photograph shows the Vectis and Isle of Wight Cycling Clubs, lined up outside the Clarendon Hotel, Shanklin, in 1900. Note the oil burning lamps on their bikes. A guide to the Island for 1906 says in its section on cycling, 'The roads are, in the main, of gravel, and owing to faulty construction and bad systems of repair the surface is often wet and muddy or very loose'.

51. *(Above)* The Congregational Chapel in the High Street, Ventnor was built 1853-54 from the designs of Mr Raffles Brown of Liverpool, at a cost of £1,800. The Rev. R. Allen, whose funeral this was, was for 40 years the pastor of the chapel.

52 & 53. *(Opposite page)* In the latter part of the 19th century the Ventnor local authority obtained a lease of some 16 acres of land from Steephill Estate and turned it into Ventnor Park, and in 1910 the town bought the freehold. One photograph shows a bicycle 'Gymkhana' in 1905, the other a parade of decorated hoops in 1906.

54. The Royal National Hospital at Ventnor was begun in 1868 from designs by the honorary architect, Thomas Hellyer of Ryde. The foundation stone of the second block to be built was laid, on behalf of Queen Victoria, by her daughter Princess Louise. In the middle of the hospital can be seen the chapel of St Luke. The Hospital has since been demolished, and the site is now occupied by a car park: it's grounds are now part of Ventnor Botanical Gardens.

55. The Sandrock mineral spring was discovered by Thomas Waterworth in 1808 and within two years he had built a well-head and a dispensary. Another person to realise that there were financial gains to be made from the spring was James Cull, a brewer of Newport. He purchased Rock Cottage which stood near the spring, enlarged it, and opened it as the Sandrock Hotel in 1818. This photograph shows it in 1904, but it has recently burnt down.

West Wight

56. The small town of Yarmouth has a long history, with its first charter in 1135. Several further charters were granted, with the final one given by James I in 1609. From then until 1891, the town was governed by a Mayor and Corporation. The size of the town can be gauged by this photograph of the hunt passing along the narrow High Street towards the Square in February 1909.

57. In the background of this photograph of The Square, Yarmouth, in the early part of the century, can be seen the parish church of St James, built in 1614. On the right, behind the carriage, is the Town Hall which was rebuilt in 1763. Markets were held on the ground floor and the Corporation met in the upper room.

58. On April 25th 1908, in a blinding blizzard, the American liner *St Paul* rammed the warship *H.M.S. Gladiator* in the Solent near Fort Victoria, to the west of Yarmouth. The liner hit the warship amidships, making a 40ft hole. The *Gladiator* drifted astern and went aground, keeling over with the loss of twenty-seven lives. This photograph shows sailors preparing to dive during the salvage operations that followed.

59. Golden Hill Fort, seen in the background, to the left of this photograph, was designed in 1863 as a defensible barrack for 136 officers and men. The roof was constructed for mounting eighteen light guns protected by earthen parapets, but in 1872 six 40 pounder guns were actually mounted. Later the fort became The Western District School for Gunnery.

60. This photograph is taken from the north side of Tennyson Down, looking north towards Totland Bay. On the extreme left can be seen the Roman Catholic chapel belonging to Weston Manor House. In the early 20th century the building was restored, after designs by A.W. Pugin, by the owner, Edward Granville Ward.

61. Bathing machines on the beach at Freshwater Bay in about 1900. In the background, hidden in the cliffs, is Freshwater Redoubt, a fort built in 1855-56. It was defended on the landward side by a deep ditch, seen on the right. On the extreme right of the photograph is the Albion Hotel which was built in the early 19th century.

62. The early years of Prince's Road, Freshwater, before proper pavements or street lighting. The camera was pointing towards the junction of Tennyson Road on the right and The Avenue on the left. Behind the fence on the right was a small brickworks.

63. Totland Bay Pier was opened in 1880 at the same time as the large hotel to the right of the photograph. The pier was 450 feet long, and built of iron and pleasure steamers from Bournemouth called in the summer season. On the extreme left, in the background, can be seen Fort Albert which was built on the beach from 1854 to 1856.

Cowes

64. The right to operate the ferry between East and West Cowes was held by the Robertson family of East Cowes in the latter half of the 18th century. In 1859 the Cowes Ferry Company took over from them and introduced steam floating bridges. The ferry in the photograph was operated by the local authority who took control in 1901, because of local dissatisfaction with the company.

65. The Parade, West Cowes, with the private landing stage of the Royal Yacht Squadron in the background. The lady (note her veil) and two children are passing the bastion which formed part of Cowes Castle, built in the 16th century. The yacht club acquired the Castle in 1857 and in the following year made it their club-house, which it still remains.

66. The Parade, Cowes, at the end of the last century. To the left is the Globe Hotel, which was in business by 1847. In the centre is the Marine Hotel where Napoleon III of France stayed in 1871.

67. The greengrocer's business of Mrs Ash, 31 Bath Road, Cowes, was the last shop before entering the High Street. Although only one person can be seen in this photograph, it would have been very busy during August with people making their way from the shops to The Parade to watch the yachting.

68 & 69. Fleet reviews have been a feature of the Solent for many years. Since the 19th century they have been held for coronations and jubilees and these photographs show the English, French and U.S.A. fleets assembled off Cowes.

70. The Victoria Pier, Cowes was built by the local council at a cost of £10,500 and opened to the public in March 1902. Pleasure steamers used it each summer, and from the seaward end of the pier there were excellent views of the harbour, passing liners and the yacht racing.

71. The White Star liner *Olympic* was only a year old when this photograph was taken in 1912. As a result of the sinking of the *Titanic* earlier in the year, extra lifeboats had been put aboard the *Olympic*, but it was claimed that they were unseaworthy. The liner sailed to an anchorage in Spithead so that they could be tested, with the result that no passengers would book a passage until new lifeboats were installed. The paddle steamer *Duchess of York* is acting as a tender.

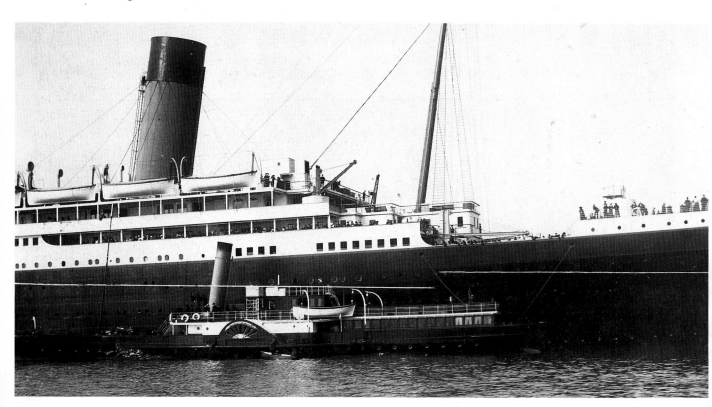

Newport and Carisbrooke

72. St Thomas' Church, Newport was designed by Samual Dawkes and built in 1854-56 on the site of a medieval church by Messrs T & J Dashwood of Ryde at a cost of £12,000. This fine photograph, possibly taken early on a Sunday morning shows the carts of various carriers who worked out of Newport to all parts of the Island.

73. Several sites for an Island memorial to Queen Victoria were considered before it was decided that it should be erected in St James' Square, Newport. It was designed by Percy Stone, a local architect and was unveiled by Princess Beatrice, the Queen's daughter, on the 13th August, 1903. On both sides of the memorial can be seen the railings of the cattle market.

74. The cattle market had been held in St James' Square for many years and attracted farmers from all over the
Island. Each year, just before Christmas, the Gilton Show was held with the prize animal having its horns
gilded.

75. The junction of Newport's High Street with Lower St James' Street and St James' Square, showing the paved crossings which allowed people to cross the road without getting their shoes muddy. The building on the right, with the large windows, was the home of the Isle of Wight County Club. In the background can be seen the Guildhall clock tower which was built in 1887 to commemorate Queen Victoria's Golden Jubilee.

76 & 77. In 1910 there were two General Elections. In January Mr Douglas Hall (Conservative) won the Island from Sir Godfrey Baring (Liberal), hanging on to the seat in the December election. The photograph above is of the declaration of the poll in the January whilst the one on the left shows the declaration of the December election from the balcony of the Town Hall.

78. The Lukely Brook from the Bowcombe Valley flows into Carisbrooke village, through the corn mill and then over this ford, before joining the River Medina in Newport. The thatched cottage was, at one time, the house of the brewer, with the brewery to the right, out of this photograph.

79. To the left of this photograph of Newport is the large Nine Acres field which was used for many events including the Royal Isle of Wight Agricultural Show. The sun has picked out St Thomas' Church, which stands proudly above the roofs of the town, and in the background is the River Medina which flows down towards Cowes. The chimney of Mew's Brewery can be seen in the centre of the photograph. Nine Acres field is now part of the playing fields of the school that commemorates its name.

80. In the Domesday Survey it was stated that the King held Alvington and that Carisbrooke Castle stood within the confines of the manor. The house is thought to be late 17th century, with later additions. When this photograph was taken in 1907, it was lived in by William Marsh, who worked the farm behind the house.

81. The Isle of Wight Foxhounds meeting in the yard of Carisbrooke Castle, with the Great Hall in the background. In the 17th century it was used by Charles I whilst he was imprisoned in the castle. During the 19th century new windows, with diamond panes, were inserted and the hall was opened to the public.

JACOB.

JACK.

82. 'Jacob' and 'Jack', the two donkeys at Carisbrooke Castle, with their keeper at the turn of the century. The Great Well in Carisbrooke Castle was said to have been dug about 1150 after the failure of the well in the keep. The well house in this photograph was built in the 16th century. Donkeys were in regular use to draw up the water buckets, by the early 18th century. Later, in the century a donkey was granted a pension of a penny loaf per day.

83. St Dominic's Priory was built in 1866 by the Countess of Clare at a cost of £18,000. The Countess is buried in the Mount Joy Cemetary which is behind the Priory. In the foreground are cannon which were brought into Carisbrooke Castle in the 19th century for training purposes by the Isle of Wight Artillery Militia.

Wootton and Havenstreet

84. The large number of followers of the local hunt, seen here crossing Wootton Bridge, gives some idea how popular the event was.

85. The road from Newport originally came down Wootton High Street, round by the front of the mill, seen on the right of this photograph, then across the bridge and up Kite Hill. In the middle of the 19th century it was decided to build a new road giving direct access to the bridge, from the High Street. This meant greatly extending the tunnels which carried the water under the road to work the mill.

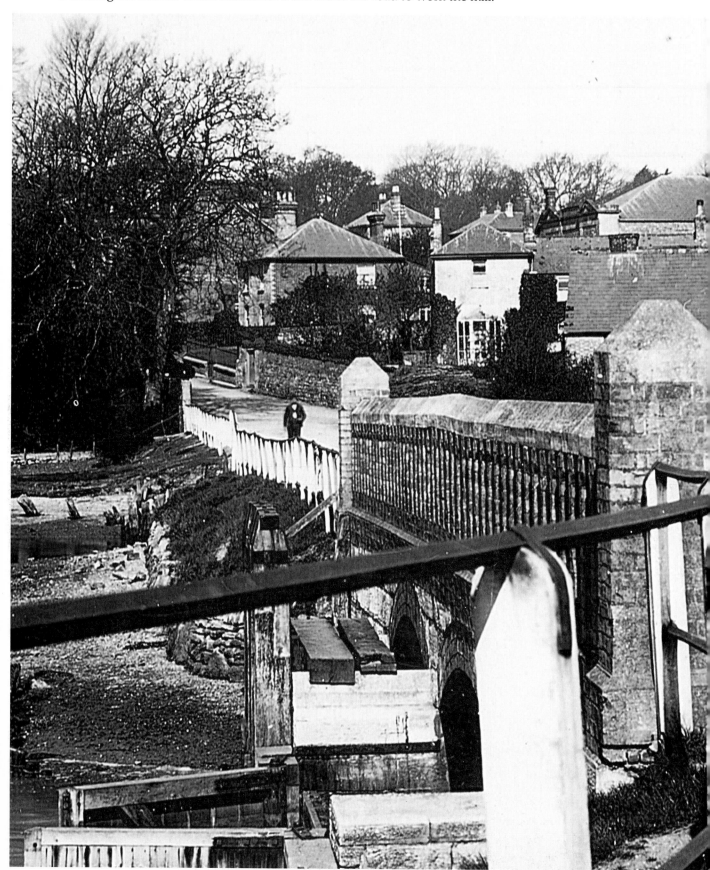

86. *(Left)* The Wootton sub-postmaster, George Mew, is seen standing outside his shop, together with his wife and daughter. Letters arrived at his office as early as 4.50 a.m. and were dispatched as late as 8.30. p.m., also the National Telephone Co. had a telephone call office here. The grocery and bakery were run by Alfred Mew.

87. *(Below)* The temporary iron church of St Michael and All Angels in Wootton Common Graveyard was demolished in 1909 and a new church dedicated to St Mark was built in Station Road, Wootton, then in the parish of Arreton. Later that area of Wootton and the new church were transferred to the parish of Wootton.

88 & 89. Fernhill House at Wootton was built in about 1792 for the Hon. Thomas Orde, later Lord Bolton, when he was Governor of the Island. It stood on high ground, surrounded by trees, with a fine view across Wootton Creek. The observatory in the glorious harvest scene was erected by the Brodie family, who owned the house when this photograph was taken.

90. Havenstreet in 1900. In the background is Havenstreet School which was built in 1892 by the Ryde School Board at a cost of £1,200. The cyclist is standing at the junction of the Main Road with Church Road.

91. Havenstreet became part of the parish of Ashey in 1853. Before then the boundary of the Newchurch and Arreton parishes had divided the village. To the left of this photograph is the White Hart Inn, with its sign hanging outside. The two storey building in the centre is the Longford Institute, built by John Rylands in 1885 for the benefit of the villagers.

92. John Rylands, a merchant from Manchester, purchased Beaulieu House, Havenstreet in 1882. It had been built in 1853 for the Rev. Kent, who was the first incumbent of the local church. John Rylands greatly enlarged the house and renamed it Longford, after his main home near Manchester. What you see here is the classic Victorian 'villa', complete with tower, conservatory, shutters and creepers.

93. Speeds, Havenstreet, near Longford House, in 1909. Speeds was in the old parish of Newchurch and was one of several small thatched farms in the area.

94. The approach to Havenstreet Station. The Station opened in *1875* when the line from Ryde to Newport was completed. The cottages to the left of the station houses workers who operated the local gas works which was situated across the line from the station. On the footpath is the station master, Frederick Deadman.

Rural Scenes.

95. This photograph showing a postman delivering the mail is one of a handful by Broderick taken on the Island that have yet to be identified. It probably dates to about 1900, when the post was both delivered and collected twice a day in even the remotest of the Isle of Wight villages.

96. The Isle of Wight Point to Point meeting at Limerston in March 1907, with its wonderful mixture of 'gentry', farmers and townsfolk out for a day in the country.

97. Sheep were a common sight roaming large areas of the downs. These, being sheared by hand at Yaverland Farm, would have grazed on the down behind the farm. An annual wool fair was held in Newport with many thousands of fleeces being sold.

98. Abraham and Jane Salter, the farmer and his wife, in their cart at Walpen Farm, Chale. They are dressed for Newport Market, probably taking (for sale) provisions, which are under the cover at the back of the cart.

99. The National School at Brighstone was built in 1835 and later enlarged to accommodate 150 children, but the average attendance was about half that number. The master, Mr Philip Lempriere is seen with some of his boys. His wife was the girls' mistress.

100. During the years before the First World War the Isle of Wight Rifles camped several times at Lock's Green, near Newtown, to use the rifle range.

101. North Court, Shorwell, one of the finest manor houses in the Island. There has been a house on the site since Domesday, but the house in the photograph is mainly 17th century and was built for Sir John Leigh. Considerable alterations were carried out in 1837 and again in 1907. In the early years of this century the house was occupied by Mrs Disney Leith, who was a friend of the poet Swinburne.

102. Godshill Park House was built in about 1850 and enlarged at the beginning of this century. In 1912, when this group had gathered to watch a meet of the Isle of Wight foxhounds, it belonged to Captain Samuel Davenport. Godshill Park had originally been part of the vast estates owned by the Worsley family, whose main seat was Appuldurcombe.

103. This photograph of the western end of Brading Down shows how open the area was in the early years of this century. In the background is Bembridge Down with the road leading up to the fort.